The Shoes I Walked In

Mission: To Proclaim Transformation and Truth

Publisher: Transformed Publishing, Cocoa, FL

Website: www.transformedpublishing.com

Email: transformedpublishing@gmail.com

Cover Design: Savion Owens savionowens19@gmail.com

This book is a memoir and not a recommended course of treatment for any mentioned life issues (relational, medical, mental, emotional, substance abuse, etc.). Characters, organizations, places, events, and incidents are described based on the author's life experiences for the sole purpose of sharing her story.

Unless otherwise noted, Scriptures are taken from New King James Version®. Copyright © 1982 by Thomas Nelson. Used by permission. All rights reserved.

As noted, NLT, Scriptures are taken from Holy Bible, New Living Translation, Copyright © 1996, 2004, 2015 by Tyndale House Foundation. Used by permission of Tyndale House Publishers, Inc., Carol Stream, Illinois 60188. All rights reserved.

As noted, ESV, Scriptures are taken from The Holy Bible, English Standard Version. ESV® Text Edition: 2016. Copyright © 2001 by Crossway Bibles, a publishing ministry of Good News Publishers.

ISBN: 978-1-953241-40-5

Based on True Life Events

The Shoes I Walked In

Dorothea Salbi

I can do all things through Christ who strengthens me.

-Philippians 4:13

Encouragement

This is not a book for you to feel sorry for me, nor is it a sympathy book. This book was written to let people know that they're not alone. It can happen to the best of us.

For I know the plans I have for you," says the Lord. "They are plans for good and not for disaster, to give you a future and a hope. In those days when you pray, I will listen. If you look for me wholeheartedly, you will find me. I will be found by you," says the Lord. "I will end your captivity and restore your fortunes. I will gather you out of the nations where I sent you and will bring you home again to your own land."

-Jeremiah 29:11-14 NLT

Acknowledgements

I would like to thank God for giving me this book to write about my life so it may help someone else. I thank my daughter, Natasha, for running across my book and letting me know, "People need to read this book because it may help someone else." I would like to thank my kids who knew this book was coming out and are not ashamed of what I have shared.

Dedication

This book is dedicated to those who prayed for me, while I was in the darkest time of my life, and those who showed me love and grace along the way.

To my mother, who took care of my kids, while I was out doing only God knows what.

To my church family, thank you all for never looking down on me and only wanting me to come back to Christ.

To Jesus, who transformed my life. Thank you, Jesus for the love, grace, and mercy You showed me, even in a world of sin when I needed it most.

Table of Contents

Introduction: My Story

It's amazing how quickly life can take a turn for the worst. One moment everything is normal; the next minute everything can change. This is a true story about turning points that happened in my life. First, I would like to say thank you to God for letting me write this book so it can heal and deliver the many people it is going to reach.

My name is Dorothea. I was born February 29, 1964, around 12:00 a.m. My mother was asked what date she wanted recorded for my birthday. They offered her a choice because I was born on a *leap day*. She could choose from the 28th, 29th, or March 1st. My mom said, "She was born on the 29th, so that's her birthday."

I grew up in a little town call Merritt Island, which is in Florida. I am the third child out of six. I was always a good little girl as far as I can remember. That's why I didn't understand things that were happening to me at such a young early age. I was lost in fear. I felt worthless, unwanted, and caught in deep darkness. I was not sure what was going on. *Was it something I did? Was it something I said? Was it the way I acted? What was it?*

I don't know what your story is or how you grew up. I'm guessing; however, you know what it means to wander in a circle, without going anywhere, feeling like you are on a merry go round. Don't get me wrong, I had some good days too, but as I look back over my life I can truly say, all my bad days outweighed my good days and still I didn't complain.

1
The Hurt

I kept the hurt and pain deep inside the shame because it went on and I didn't stop it. I started thinking it was my fault. As I sit here and think back, I remember the hurt. *What if I had just told someone?*

I struggled to know who I really was. *Was I put here for this? Why won't it stop? Why is this happening?*

Some hurt runs deeper than you can ever imagine. The greatest pain I have experienced in my life was a result of something that never should have occurred in the first place. Something I had no control over.

This is the kind of hurt that comes back every now and then, surpassing childhood and far into adulthood. I can pinpoint my *hurt* to the early age of four when a family member sexually molested me. Because it was a relative of mine, I was frequently at their house. It happened every time I went over there. I didn't like going, but every weekend I was sent. I cried but there was nothing I could do. *Why didn't anyone notice? Why didn't anyone see? Why didn't anyone ask? Why didn't anyone care? God, why didn't You show them I was hurting, and I was in pain?* I often said, "Remember, little children shouldn't have to go through this."

I vividly remember where *it* first happened - in a trailer. It was red and white. The exact room was off to the right. There was no door, just a curtain. One time I looked over and there was blood in a metal can of hair grease. I can still picture the details of the label in my mind. My blood was sitting on top of the grease in the can. I guess that's when he broke me.

I just want to know why he did this to me. Why? Can someone please tell me, why? He took something I was to save for my husband. I would never know or feel how it is to make love for the first time with someone special.

The saddest part about this whole thing is one of my other relatives walked in the room that day. He was caught and only asked, "What are you doing to her?" I was told to put on my clothes and go outside to play. No one ever asked me, not even once, if I was alright. The witness never said anything to anyone nor called the police.

4

Maybe you have also suffered physical and / or sexual abuse from people who were supposed to love and care for you. If that's what love is, I can do without it. *Why is it that too often, family members hurt us the most?* Through all of this, I also dealt with other family members who were mean as snakes to me. They were mentality and physically abusive.

At the age of five, I was made to eat on the floor with my face toward the corner of the wall. I was told, "You are too ugly to look at and no one wants to see your face." *How is that for a kick in the heart?*

One summer, my brother and I had to stay at an abusive family member's house. My mom was out of town. There was a particular time when my brother didn't wash his butt good, so I had to wash out his under clothes. To remind you, I was only five years old at the time. I was given a stool to reach the sink. I had to use the bathroom, so I got down and told her I had to pee. She told me, "Go back and do as I told you!" I began to wet myself. I began to cry. When I told her I had wet myself, she got so mad. I went to get the mop to clean it up. She asked me, "What are you doing?"

"I'm going to get it up," I explained.

"Lick it up!" she hollered.

I looked at her and quickly realized, she was not playing. She was serious. I began to lick it up. I guess I was going too slow, so she began to beat me with a belt buckle until I passed out. I woke up as the ambulance driver was removing me from the home.

When we used to eat, and I would hit the spoon on the plate, she would say, "Who is the one scraping my flowers off my plate?" Then she would take the plate and send me to bed hungry.

The only good thing I can remember is every February 29th, she would bake me a cake. She must have felt guilty because that's the only nice thing she ever did for me.

They were the adults. How could they do this? They knew it was wrong.

As I got older, I loved her. *Why? I don't know!* However, my brother on the other hand, who they treated like a king, couldn't stand them. Funny the way things work out. The one she almost beat to death, grew up to love her. The one they loved so much, grew up not to care much for them.

My brother and I have the same father. We often stayed the weekend together. He was loved and I was hated because my brother looked just like our dad, and I didn't.

The relative that molested me died when I was sixteen, so I never found out why he did what he did to me. When I first heard about his death, I wasn't sad. I was happy. I hate to say it but it's true. I was actually joyful.

Sometimes I wonder, *How many other kids did he do this to? Or was it only me?* I saw him once when I was about ten years old. He never looked me in the face. *What was he thinking?* I bet I know. *Does she remember?* Yes, I did.

Once I started to go to school, I didn't stay with them every weekend. That was a release. Soon I stopped going altogether to this relative's house. I was so happy.

Unfortunately, my relief didn't last for too long. I went to Melbourne, about forty minutes away from Merritt Island, with one of my cousins for the summer and the molestation started again. It didn't continue on as long as the first one.

The first time it happened with him I was asleep. He came in and began to rape me. My body began to react as though I enjoyed it. I feel like that made him think he could do it again.

7

Another late night, when he tried to come in my room again, my cousin caught him and beat him with a broom stick. To avoid being abused, I started pushing the dresser behind the door at night so he couldn't get in. I waited to go to sleep until the morning when my cousin was awake. Because he smelled like onions, I hated that smell for a long time. The smell of onions automatically reminded me of him.

He eventually passed away. It may sound harsh, and even a little cruel, but I was happy he was gone. Now, I wouldn't have to worry about the things he was doing to me or someone else.

I was sad growing up as a little girl. I questioned a lot of things. *God, why me? Does anyone love me or care enough about me to see the things going on in my life? I am a child.* I was emotionally stabbed in the heart, when I was told by someone who was supposed to love me, "I wish you were never born."

This may be hard to understand, but some teenagers who have been sexually molested become very sexually active. Please don't look at them as *being grown, fast,* or *hot in the tail.* Their hypersexuality, may be a result of what they were introduced to at an early age. Not by choice, but by force. When no one intervened, it may have become right in their eyes because it was allowed to happen to them. Some never told because they were afraid of what might happen next.

Many of you reading this, have suffered your own kind of hurt and heart damage. Like me, you may have been sexually abused as a child. I have read statistics that say one in four girls and one in six boys will be abused either physically, sexually, and / or mentally, before the age of eighteen.

I have a message to every reader who has been emotionally abused by listening to a lot of negative ideas about yourself from your parents, aunts, uncles, or anyone else growing up. Also, to those who have been betrayed by people they trusted to protect them. Please know there is a God who sits high and looks down low.

... But God

But God loves us so much that He gave His one and only Son for us (*see* John 3:16). Yes, even the ones who violated you, as payment for our sins. He cares for us so much. No matter what we've done, or what has been done to us, and again them who did it too, He still welcomes *us* as His sons and daughters. When negative circumstances show up in our lives, we must be willing to look for God's direction in the midst of losing and finding our way. In some of our situations, we come to a point where we seem to hit a dead end in the road. We can't back up. We can't turn around. There's no way out. The only way of escape is to call a tow truck (Jesus). These things may come suddenly and unexpectedly, like turning a corner and running into a brick wall, but make sure not to fall.

2

Even When

Even when I was a little girl,
I was born in this evil world

Even when I was a little girl,
I had no life among the wolves

Even when I was a little girl,
I wanted to commit suicide

Even when I was a little girl,
because all the pain that was inside

Even when I was a little girl,
I felt no love

Even when I was a little girl,
no not even from above

Even when I was a little girl,
I was all alone

Even when I was a little girl,
I was wronged

By Dorothea

I never told my mother what happened to me as a little girl. I guess I was scared I would get in trouble. I can't remember her telling us to let her know if anyone ever touches us. I do remember her telling my sister, "If you call yourself having sex, I'm going to kill you." Now I know it to be abuse, but since it was sex, I kept it from her.

When I entered junior high school, I started being bullied by a group of girls. They were bigger than I was and could fight. See, I was never the kind to fight. Instead, I brought money and candy to school to keep them from beating me up. I was only safe when my two friends came to school. They knew not to try them because they would give *it* to them. When they said they were going to fight me after school, I would run off the bus as soon as it came to a stop, all the way home. They couldn't catch me.

Until one day I had to fight. They pushed their sister to fight me, and we started to fight. I was doing everything I knew how to. I pulled her shirt. Her breast came out. As she was trying to hide her breast, I took the opportunity to put it on her real good. I was winning. Someone grabbed me and held me. My head was down. She kicked me in the nose, and it started to bleed. *Why would they do that? Why?*

It didn't end there. I still had problems, but they knew if I was backed into a corner I would fight. Whenever I would get into a fight, it was like being molested and abused all over again. I started carrying a knife and a bottleneck. For those who don't know what a bottleneck is, it is literally the neck of a beer bottle. I would use it, could use it, and was good at using it.

It is bad enough when a nonmember of your family abuses you, but a close relative is the worst. When a girl is molested at a young age, she begins to discharge because her body has been introduced to sex (like a woman but still a little girl). I was watching TV when someone called me outside. Some boys had my panties and were throwing them around. Someone close to me gave my panties to them. I was hurt and ashamed. I cried as they threw them in the air from one to the other.

There was this lady who lived close by us. She saw what they were doing. Not to say too much, but they got the worst butt cutting they ever had. The one who *should* have fought for me was in on it as well. I got him back though, and good. Let's just say they *knew* the next time.

My sister got pregnant with her first child when she was fifteen years old. I overheard a conversation between my mother and a lady in our neighborhood. She asked my mother if my sister was pregnant. My mother answered, "Yes, I should kick her off the porch." I didn't know how powerful words could really hurt until I heard *those* words. Proverbs 18:21 says, "Death and life are in the power of the tongue, and those who love it will eat its fruit."

I started running away when I was fourteen years old trying to be *hot in the butt*. My mother would find me and take me back home and beat me. She wasn't wrong. This would be the first of many butt cuttings. When she would get ready to beat me, I would run out the door like a jack rabbit running from a wolf. She would get my brothers to hold me because she knew I would run but I would bite them and get away. She told them, "If she gets away, I'm going to beat both of you!"

One time I was getting a beating and tried to run. She caught me by the shirt and slung me down the hall. I hit my head on the corner of the door. Blood went everywhere.

Another time she beat me with a school paddle my brother made in his shop class. She beat me for so long and so hard, a blister formed on my butt. It looked like someone took a hot iron and placed it on me and left it. I couldn't sit down right for about a week. She didn't send me to school the next couple of days.

Don't get me wrong, my mom was a great woman. That was just the way she chastised us when we were doing wrong.

I used to take things out of stores. I don't know if I did this because of what happened to me or if I was crying out for help. *Only God knows.*

3

Me Becomes We

I didn't have many friends in high school; however, I did have one. She was definitely a true friend. When the other kids' moms stopped them from hanging around me when I got pregnant at an early age, her mother didn't stop her from being my friend. I am sure the other kids got pregnant also, but their parents just got them abortions. My mom didn't believe in that. She said, "If you laid there and got it, you will lay there and have it."

I was pregnant at the age of fifteen while still in school. The boy was seventeen. He told his parents the baby was not his. He was my first boyfriend, but I wasn't a virgin. Like I said in the beginning of this book, my uncle broke me and put my blood in a metal can. He took from me what I was supposed to give to my husband. So, you can say my own uncle was my first, but *not* my first love. My uncle was actually my first rape, which lowered my self-esteem. A lot of tears have flowed for some time, . . . *But God.*

As if one teenage pregnancy wasn't enough, I got pregnant by the same guy again at the age of seventeen. My first child was a girl and next came a little boy. I was so in love, actually young and stupid. I didn't want to listen to Mama. She plainly told me, "That boy don't mean you any good!" Me and my kids' father broke up. He went on to get married, have more kids, and never had anything to do with *our* kids.

He once told my mother he just wanted to forget he ever had our kids. In his own words, "He put them on the back burner like eyes on the stove." *How can a man forget about his first kids? His first daughter and his first son. A real man wouldn't but a boy would.*

I began to date again, and I thought *he* was the one until one night I went to his house to see him. He had some of his friends over, so I just went into the room like always. But this time it was different. He came into the room. We made love. Then he left the room like he was going to get some water. A few minutes after he left the room, *they* came in one after another and raped me. I didn't do anything because I was afraid of dying.

How can men be so cruel knowing they have sisters, aunts, and a mother? What if someone had done this to a female who is some kin to them?

When they finished, I put on my clothes. As I went through the living room, with my head down, they laughed. I left. As I got down the road, my *boyfriend* came running behind me. I was scared. He asked me if I was going to tell anyone. I said, "No, I've been through it all my life." I saw this guy again maybe once or twice. He just passed me with his head hanging down.

As I write this book, I cry. Tears roll down my face. The shame kept me quiet but now it's time for the healing process to begin in my life. This book is not about anyone but me, some will like it, and some won't.

The next man I met was *the woman beater.* Let me just say this: any man who beats a woman is scared of a man. I had two kids with him. Our first child was born in 1983 and the second in 1984. He was good to me. He gave me money. He also took care of my two kids who weren't his. But baby let me tell you, he was a wolf in sheep's clothing.

He was a woman beater, more accurately a horror. He locked me up when he went to work. I remember one time he beat me for about an hour with an exercise bar. I had bruises everywhere. He also had a girlfriend downstairs from me. If I said anything to him about it, he would beat me. He gave me STDs. I was at the clinic at least two or three times a month.

We moved into another apartment complex in Merritt Island. Some girl moved in next door to us with her cousin. Her cousin treated her bad and wouldn't even let her cook food for her kids. Check this out, I let her cook for her kids and bathe them over at my house. Well, you guessed it, her and him started seeing each other right under my nose. I left and moved out. He moved in with her.

I got pregnant by him again in 1985. He said he didn't want any more kids. He came over one day with some wine, so I thought. A couple of weeks later I started getting sick. My cousin called me and said don't drink that wine. It was too late. I had already drunk some. I started losing parts of the baby. I had to terminate the pregnancy.

It took me a while to forgive him for that, but it took me longer to forgive myself. I found out the other girl was pregnant. I never thought he would do all that he did to me.

I was afraid of him. When he hit me, I wouldn't fight back. But one day, after everything he put me through, I got tired of him. I laid into him with a beer bottleneck. I cut him three inches from his heart. That's when I made up my mind to leave him alone because the next time he hit me, I might have killed him.

4

Not Again

One night I was bathing my oldest daughter. She was four years old at the time. The same age I was when *it* started to happen to me. I wiped her private part, and she acted like it hurt. I asked her what was wrong. She looked afraid to tell me. I told her it was going to be alright. It was not her fault. She told me her uncle on her daddy's side had done *it*.

I called her father immediately and told him what she told me. He said he didn't believe her. I didn't understand why he couldn't believe it. I had already caught the same brother having sex with his other niece when my daughter was a baby. I blame myself because I let her go over there with her father. *It* happened to my own child.

The kicker is a couple weeks later he called me to tell me they caught his brother doing the same thing to another niece. I said to him, "I guess you feel like a real butthole," and hung up my phone. I pressed charges against him, but when we went to court, they dropped the charges and let him go because she was too small to testify. He passed away years later never asking her or me to forgive him for what he had done to her.

Let Go

It is time to let go of the pain,
it is time to let go because
you have so much to gain.

It is time to let go of the hurt,
it is time to get rid of the dirt.

It is time to hold on to God's
unchanging hand, and forgive
those who tried to mess up God's
plan. It is time to let go and
forgive yourself because it is
for you and no one else.

By Dorothea

My son told me it happened to him also. He didn't tell me until he was older though. He said every time he showered, his uncle would come in and molest him. All I could do was cry. *How could I have not seen the signs of what was going on? What was wrong with me? How could I have been so stupid?*

When you come out from under the umbrella of God and go into the storm, there is no covering. For years, since the age of eleven, I had been in the church. Then I decided to try the world. I used to get high right across the street from where I went to church. I would hide to keep my family from seeing me. *How many know you can hide from man, but you can't hide from God?*

I got high one time for about four days and nights. Nonstop. Nothing but smoking, eating little and drinking much. Next thing I knew, my body gave out; I dropped. I was awakened by a drug dealer. He could have had sex with me or allowed other men to, but he didn't. He watched over me all night. Later the next morning, he told me to go home, and I didn't need to be out here.

How many of you know that God will send you an angel to watch over you in your darkest time? God was my light in the darkness when I couldn't see my way. I thank God even when I was lost, He let me find my way back home. Psalm 119:105 tells me, God's word is a lamp to my feet, and a light for my path.

Outside of God, all I found was hurt, disappointment, misuse, all kinds of abuse, and mental instability. But I can truly admit, no matter the lightning, no matter the thunder, and how the rain fell, God was there all along.

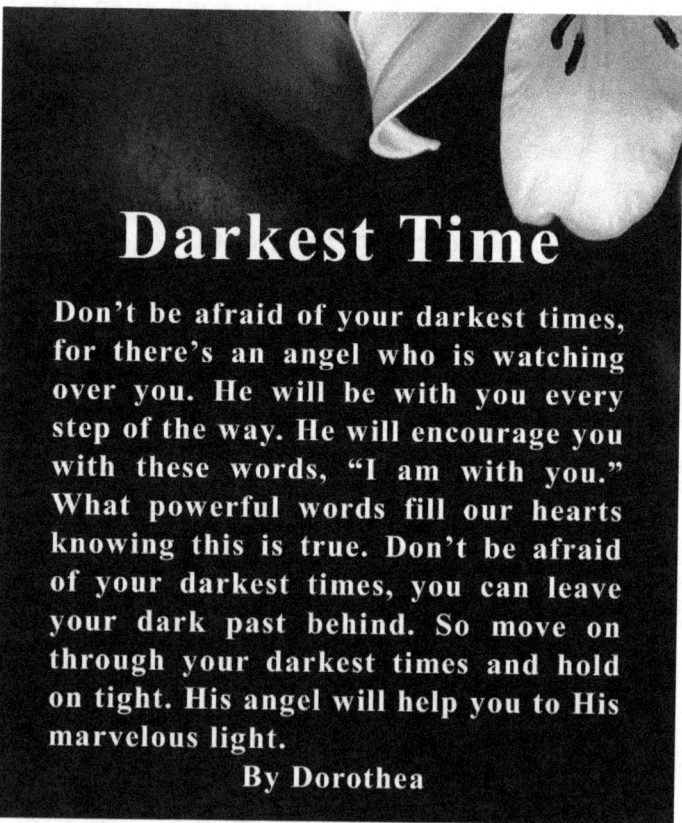

Darkest Time

Don't be afraid of your darkest times, for there's an angel who is watching over you. He will be with you every step of the way. He will encourage you with these words, "I am with you." What powerful words fill our hearts knowing this is true. Don't be afraid of your darkest times, you can leave your dark past behind. So move on through your darkest times and hold on tight. His angel will help you to His marvelous light.

By Dorothea

5

Let the Drugs Begin

In 1985, after losing my baby, along with all the other stuff that was happening and going on in my life, I was introduced to crack cocaine. The first time I used crack it felt good. I did not know this drug was about to tear my life, my family, and my kids' lives apart.

I quickly found out about the white horse I heard about when I was a little girl. An apostle said there would be a white horse that would come to Merritt Island, and it would look like a ghost town. Some of the people under his voice hit the highway of destruction in our small town. Little did I know when I heard the word, that it would hit my home, and *it* was crack cocaine.

My world was gone. My life was about to end as I once knew it. All the hurt I was feeling, rooted in childhood pain from the rapes, beatings, and mind games pursued me into adulthood. I hid all that trauma in crack. This drug became my everything.

I met my husband in 1986. He was a great man. He didn't know I was on drugs. He was from Morocco. He was the best thing that happened to me, and I still treated him like he wasn't anything. When you have had so many bad men in your life you don't know how to treat a good one when he comes. Growing up without a father doesn't help. Not seeing how a man is supposed to treat a woman and only seeing the bad in men, never the good, doesn't help either. He was good to me, really good. I realize that now. As I look back over my life, knowing what I know now, I would have done things differently. But you must understand crack had a hold on me and my life. It is the devil in a solid white form.

All of us who were on drugs were actually walking around slowly committing suicide without even realizing it. I was doing anything and everything to get it. I was sleeping with men and women. When you're on drugs, you have no shame, until you come down from the high. That is when the shame comes in. I sold my food stamps and my kids' new clothes their father bought them. I didn't care. I just wanted to get high. If anyone ever tells you they never did anything to get drugs, they are lying. I know, I've been there. They are only saying that because they are ashamed. Not me, though. I did what I did. *Who can judge me? But God!* He is the only one who has hell or heaven to put me in.

In 1987, I became pregnant with my fifth child. He wasn't my husband's baby. My cousin helped to make sure the other side of my son's family knew him. Because my husband was a real man, he stayed with me despite my adultery. Let me tell you a little more about my husband. He married me with four kids and loved them like they were his own.

I was on crack so bad my kids and my baby were taken from me by family and children's services when a lady called the police on me. My children were placed with my mom. You would think after my children were taken, I would get it together, but I didn't because I knew they were in good hands. I was now free to get high, go where I wanted, and still able to see my kids whenever I got ready to. I believe if my kids would have been in foster care, I would have gotten myself together and gotten them back sooner.

I love my kids but at the time I was going through something called *life*. I used *it* as an excuse to do drugs and cover up all that had happened to me in my past. We must deal with our past to have a great future.

My kids were aged seven, six, five, four, and five months old when my mother got them. My husband and I moved to Atlanta, GA, with my sister and my children remained in FL with my mother. Instead of getting better, everything got worse. I would go out and stay out night after night, not knowing where I was, and let so called *men* sell me so we could get high. I know it was wrong but in the drug life, there's no right or wrong. It is just about the drugs. Life went on like that for a while.

I stayed away for weeks at a time. Finally, I would go back home to my husband, rest up, and head back out again. He never left my side. Eventually, we moved into our own place. He went to Morocco for a visit. While he was gone, I sold our new furniture and set up the house like someone had broken in. Then I called the police and filed a report to give my husband when he got back.

I was a walking time bomb ready to blow. I would have made a good extra on Michael Jackson's Thriller video. My weight dropped to ninety two pounds from one hundred eighty five pounds walking the streets, jumping in and out of cars to go with different people . . . husbands, some of their wives, people I knew, and some I didn't. None of that made a difference. The drugs were my boss, and I was their employee.

Crack has no feelings. It is a sickness. It had ahold of my soul, my body, and my mind. When you're on drugs, you work for the drug dealers. Every dime you get, you give it to them.

Sure enough, I started sleeping around with a drug dealer. Now I could get high for free, so I thought. I wasn't free. He was a woman beater, and he was a mess. I left a good man for a bad man. One night his house got busted. I went to jail. He told the cops the drugs were mine. When I went to court, they let me know they found twenty-eight pieces of crack. I told the lawyer they were not mine. I told them, "I smoke crack. If the crack was mine, you would have only found one because the other twenty-seven would have been gone."

I called my husband. He was right by my side even after everything I had done to him, he was there. He got me a lawyer and made sure I didn't want for anything while I was in jail for five months. All that time he waited for me. *Boy, was I stupid.* He took me back right after I got out of jail.

I became pregnant with our first child. This one was his little girl. We named her Esther after my mother. She looked just like him. He was so proud. We stayed together for about four more years. I was still on and off drugs. He couldn't take it anymore and he left. *Who could blame him? Nobody. Not even me.* When anyone would ask me why I left my husband, I let them know he left me, and took responsibility for my role - *it was all me.*

At the time, I didn't care. At the time, crack was my man, and *he* fulfilled all my needs. When you're on drugs, sex is the farthest thing from your mind. You do it, get up, and get high.

Now that I'm clean, I wish he was my husband. But life goes on. I had my chance. I wish him the best. I will always love him for how he treated me and the kids even when they weren't his.

6

As My World Turns

My life was about to turn upside down. The enemy was out to kill me. He decided to let me kill myself. I was headed straight for destruction. I went into abandon buildings to have sex with different kinds of men, black or white, I didn't care. I knew once I got finished, I was going to get my money, so I could get high. Like I said at the beginning of this book, I was committing suicide and didn't even know it, or just didn't care.

I went to trick with a guy at his house. When we got finished, he said his drugs were missing. I didn't take them, but he thought I did. He pulled out a gun, put it to my forehead, and pulled the trigger. It didn't go off. *Can you say, "But God?"* The clip fell on the floor. I could see a bullet in the chamber. God saved my life. Again, grace and mercy covered me. Jesus Christ's blood saved me and protected me.

That incident didn't stop me. I continued to live a *risk-taking* life. I smoked and tricked for years. I sold my food stamps and body. I cleaned people's houses even though some of them talked to me any kind of way. I didn't care. All I wanted to do was get high and stay high. When I came down, I cried because the shame kicked in.

I would stop for about a year and start back as soon as I felt the urge come back. I would begin to go back to church, clean myself up, do good, and then fall right back into active addiction. You know what the Bible says about evil spirits coming back stronger when you go back into the world - it is true.

> "When an unclean spirit goes out of a man, he goes through dry places, seeking rest; and finding none, he says, 'I will return to my house from which I came.' And when he comes, he finds it swept and put in order. Then he goes and takes with him seven other spirits more wicked than himself, and they enter and dwell there; and the last state of that man is worse than the first."
>
> -Luke 11:24-26

I moved back to Florida, got into project housing close to my kids, and kept doing what I was doing. I have tricked the best of them; big time drug dealers and white men with good jobs who worked at The Cape and The Air Force Base. Whatever I did, I was good at it - the best. They would call my phone and I would meet them wherever they told me to. Looking back now, I realize they could have been killers or rapists. *God, thank you for looking out for me and all those who are lost.*

I took my last baby to my mother. I knew it was getting bad, so before they could come take her, I gave her to my mom and lost my project housing. I would go to my mama's house and stay there when I was tired or wanted to spend time with my kids. They were still my babies and I loved them. I had it good. That's how it looked to me. That drug will have you thinking all kind of crazy.

I lost myself in drugs. I forfeited my self-respect, my self-esteem, and my self-will to the enemy. My kids didn't respect me anymore, yet they still loved me because I am their mother. I look back now and can see I chose my drugs over my kids. Tears fill my eyes when I think about all the time I gave up that could have been better spent with my babies.

7

The Men

This chapter is about the men I was with and to show you how important it is to make loving yourself first a priority. I was looking for love because I just wanted to be wanted. I had to learn to understand the unconditional love I was seeking, can only be found in Christ Jesus. It does not exist outside of Him.

Surprise, I met a man who also did drugs. It is a big mistake for two people who do drugs to be together. People tried to warn me about this fool, but I didn't listen. Boy, was I in for hell. We were together about a month. He was the devil from hell, another woman beater. He would beat me if the wind blew wrong. I remember one time we were sitting on the porch in the front yard. A car came by, the men spoke, and I waved. When he came back over to me, he said the man told him we were sleeping together. That was a lie. I told him let's go ask him, but he wouldn't. Instead, he started hitting me. He held me down and sprayed roach spray in my mouth, then he bent me over his knee. I heard something crack in my back. He dropped me. I couldn't move. He kicked me with his steel toe boots and said, "Bit$%&, get up!" I couldn't feel anything. He left me on the floor and told his grandfather, who was half blind, to come take care of me, but he couldn't do anything for me. I didn't see him again until the next morning. I was temporarily paralyzed.

He beat me a lot. I can remember another time when he was in one of his moods. I ran outside with only a towel on, and I got away from him. I went home to my mother's house. He had hit me so hard in my chest I could barely breathe. My breathing was so shallow, I had to go to the hospital. My brothers wanted to hurt him badly. My mother told them not to get involved because all I was going to do is go back with him. She was right. I did, two weeks later. He ended up shocking me and I finally got fed up and left him. I was done.

I was doing "good" by myself. I went over to another guy's house to buy some drugs. Well, my ex saw me. Mind you, he was going with another girl, but he came over there and started with me. He picked up a table and threw it at me. He hit me in the head with a glass ash tray. I guess he was mad because I broke up with him.

I went into my purse, pulled out a bottleneck, and started cutting him like I would fillet a fish. He ran. I was right behind him like we were running track. Afterward, they told me he ended up with twenty stitches in his face and eight staples down his right arm, the same one he hit me with. I still see him from time-to-time walking or riding his bike. Believe it or not, he says, "You know I still love you."

With a smile on my face, I respond, "I still love you, too."

I wouldn't date him if I was Eve, he was Adam, and we were still living without sin. Amen!

Despite all I went through, I was still doing drugs, while looking and trying to find real love. Nonetheless, I only ended up with women beaters. My husband was the only real man who I wholeheartedly loved, but I didn't want him. *Was it because of what happened to me? Or was it because of the lack of love in my past? Is that why I didn't know real love when it came?*

When we as women, look for love in all the wrong places, we end up with all the wrong men. Take my advice, "Don't look for love. Let love find you." The Bible says in Proverbs 18:22, "He who finds a wife finds a good thing, and obtains favor from the Lord." Not, *she* find a husband. Keep that in mind ladies.

Along came a man who ended up becoming my best friend. *He was cool to be a white guy.* He would come get me and we would hang out. He didn't do drugs. He was just a freak. You must know one thing about him, he had prostate cancer so he couldn't get it up, if you know what I mean. He had to give himself a shot to get a feeling. All I had to do is pinch him and hit him hard.

Like I said, he became my best and dearest friend. We used to go fishing and crabbing together. He would call me to make sure I'm doing good. He told me every day how proud he was of me. He said I guess if God did that, then He's okay. He was an atheist, but God moved in his life. It's funny how you meet a person doing the wrong thing and they end up being your best friend. I love that man. I could talk to him about anything. I was friends with him through three heart surgeries and two pacemakers. We had an over twenty-year friendship. In 2015, I lost my best friend. He loved me so much. He told me at the time of his first heart surgery, he was going to leave me something if anything ever happened to him. Well, when he passed, he left me fifteen thousand dollars. To this day, I truly miss him.

Then there was an older guy, who was twenty-three years my senior who I met in 1996 hanging out under the tree. People went under *this* tree to play cards, drink, buy drugs, sell food, find men to trick with, etc. This particular man had a very nasty mouth when it came to me. He would say things like, "I wouldn't have a woman like you," meaning a woman on drugs. And, "I'll take you and pimp you out." He was a man with plenty of money. He liked putting people down and looked down on people because he felt he was better than others.

Well, one day I was walking down the street to get my medication (if you know what I mean). Here came mister high roller. Now, he wanted to get with me. With a smile on my face, I said, "No, not you. What happened to 'you wouldn't have a woman like me'?"

He had nothing to say. I told him to go to hell. The next day he was under the tree selling out. I put him out there. I told everyone around how he tried to pick me up and I told him, "No."

"That's a lie, I wouldn't go to bed with nothing like you," he said trying to plead his case.

He ran behind me for about six months. He paid people to come tell me *this and that* and to meet him *here or there*. Each time I said, "No."

One day, on my daily walk to buy my medication, again came mister high roller. I rolled my eyes, as if to say, *what do you want now?* I thought to myself, *let me show him something.* I went home with him. We did it. I wanted to make sure he knew, *if* I wanted to go to bed with him, he would.

Guess what? I couldn't get rid of him. We stayed together for about fifteen years. During this time, I moved back to Atlanta. I met another guy there. He was alright, until one day, he came out of the closet and told me he was on drugs. The door opened wide. He smoked more than I did so you know I couldn't deal with him. We stayed together for about three years. He had to go, too. He also was a woman beater. It was like I had, *I love woman beaters*, written on my forehead. *That's a lie.*

I went back home to Florida. That's when I started getting sick and went to the hospital. The stuff we put in the crack pipe messed up the lining in my stomach. I didn't care. I kept doing drugs, and still did what I had to do to get it.

It had been about two years since I saw mister high roller. We started dating as a couple. I stopped smoking for about six months, until I went to a club, started drinking, and went back on crack.

My man from Atlanta was still around all this time. He knew I was back on drugs, but he stayed right there. I told him what had happened to me as a little girl. I thought he stayed because he felt sorry for me, but he had fallen in love with me and I with him.

I began to get really sick again and went back to the hospital. I weighed ninety-two pounds and looked as if I was dead. All they had to do was put the dirt on me. I told myself, "When I get out of here, I'm not going to smoke anymore." Even I knew that was a lie when I said it. I would smoke and ask God to take *it* from me, all at the same time. I got sick again and again. After the first time I was hospitalized, I ended up in and out of the hospital. This is when I believe God began to work on my deliverance.

You might not understand this, but the sicker I got the more I smoked. I would still go to church from time to time. I didn't care how I looked because I knew, *couldn't no one judge me but God.* My church was not like that though.

They were just happy to see me any way I showed up. *This* church was about love. My pastor at the time, used to tell them, "Dorothea doesn't come to church that often, but when she does come, she praises God more than the members who come all the time." Now that I think about it, you know they say, "When praises go up, blessings come down," along with deliverance, healing, etc. You see God never leaves us, we leave him. Even in the darkest times of our lives, He will be right there.

["]Be strong and courageous. Do not fear or be in dread of them, for it is the Lord your God who goes with you. He will not leave you or forsake you."
-Deuteronomy 31:6 ESV

I was going through life not caring if I lived or died. I needed help. I couldn't do it on my own. God always hears your cries for help even if you don't think He does. Your prayers have already been answered; just keep believing. I finally found true love in a real man. His name is Jesus Christ. He gave His life for mine and gave me a chance for eternal life. Like I said at the beginning of this chapter, all I had to do was *let* God love me.

How can we, as women, love someone when some of us don't even love ourselves? Some of you might say, "I love myself," but are bearing all kinds of negative *stuff* from people - men specifically. You don't have to. Let God show you real love, true love, the best love anyone can ever show you. There's a song I recommend by Mary J. Blige called, *Good Morning Gorgeous*. Listen to it. Self-love is the best love. God showed me, all I have to do is let Him love me, with His unconditional love. The greatest love ever, is the love of God.

8

The Turn Around

God is our refuge and strength, a very
present help in the time of trouble.

-Psalm 46:1

God will give you strength to cope with what
you're going through. You get power in your
trials. Look at *going through*, as a turning point
in your life for hope, faith, and deliverance.

I called my pastor because I felt I needed
prayer. She came and got me. She prayed for me.
That's when God showed her all the things I had
been through as a little girl and young woman. I
never told her anything, but God knew. We went
to my mother's house. She sat down with my
mom and told her what God had shown her. My
pastor told my mother, "You never know what
people have been through to cause them to do the
things they do."

My mom asked me who had done it. I told her
the names of the two people. She said she
believed our cousin did it, but not my uncle on

my daddy's side. It still brings tears to my eyes now, but because of God, I made it through all the heartache, all the pain, all the guilt, all the shame, and all the unforgiveness that had me bound. I let it go and God gave me back my joy, my peace, and my deliverance was on its way.

Deliverance didn't happen overnight, especially *not* that night. I used the fact that my mom didn't believe me as another excuse to keep smoking crack. In life people find many reasons to do many things. That's why we shouldn't hold on to things that will keep us bound. We need to hold on to new stuff, like God's word, prayer, and fasting. These things will keep you from looking back at the past and moving forward to your future. The only time you should look back at your past is to see how far the Most High has brought you. Amen.

I was sick and tired of being sick and tired. You see, I was a back slider so I knew how to get back to God, but the sickness wouldn't let me. Crack cocaine is like a medication you have to have to feel better. I wasn't ashamed anymore. I started walking the street in the daytime. I didn't care who saw me anymore, family members or church members.

Here I am. . .

God, here I am;
do with me as You will

> God, here I am;
> help me to yield

God, here I am;
help me to see

> God, here I am;
> what do You
> want for me

God, here I am;
help me to pray

> God, here I am;
> help me to stay

God, here I am;
help me to fast

> God, here I am;
> help me to last

God, here I am;
I give my life to You

> God, here I am;
> use me the way You want to
> & wash me through and through.
> God, here I am.

By Dorothea

Remember the prophecy spoken by the apostle I mentioned before about the white horse? That which was spoken in 1975, was coming to pass. My community looked like a ghost town. Even church people who were under the sound of the apostle's voice were now caught up on the highway of destruction, including me.

The Highway

The highway of destruction is where the devil wanted me.

The highway of destruction is where God set me free.

The highway of destruction is where I had so much pain.

The highway of destruction is where freedom rings.

The highway of destruction is where I tried to take my life.

The highway of destruction is where I found Jesus Christ.

By Dorothea

The last time I got sick and went to the hospital, my brother came to see me. He asked me, "Do you see yourself?"

"I know," was all I could say.

The same day God told me, "If you forgive them, I'll take it away." Unforgiveness will hold you back, hold you down, and hold you up from the purpose God has for you.

I woke up one day at home. I was filled with so much joy in my heart. I remember going into the hospital, but I don't remember coming home. All I remember is walking outside and there was my friend. I hugged him. I just wasn't the same. It was as if I had lived someone else's life. I felt like I was in a dream. God had taken the drugs and alcohol from me. I could still remember I used to do drugs, but God took away the *feeling*.

I used crack for fifteen to twenty years of my life, on and off. Drugs were my crutch to support the weight of molestation and abuse I was carrying. God said to me, "I will take those crutches from you. Don't you know I kept You for just this reason . . . when they see you, they will see Me (God). Just forgive those who hurt you then forgive yourself. It wasn't your fault. I will lift your pain and hurt. I will remove the guilt you feel in your heart and put love and joy in its place."

I gave it all to God because when God speaks, you can trust His word. He is God. He cannot and will not lie. That day I didn't feel the same anymore. I felt new all through my body. It was the cleanest I ever felt. My body, mind, and soul were new.

Remember I told you I was down to weighing ninety-two pounds? I went to the doctor two weeks later. I was up to one hundred fifty pounds. My friend hung in there every step of the way. He didn't give up on me through it all; he was my king. My kids looked at me in amazement - *our mother is back after all those years she was not a part of our lives.* I was back, but by this time they were already adults. Thankfully, I didn't totally miss them growing up. Unfortunately, I wasn't there all the time either.

My kids now had kids of their own. At this time, my oldest daughter had one child, my second oldest son and my second daughter both had three children, my third daughter was in the army and pregnant with her first child, and my other two were still in school.

I wasn't there like I should have been when they were small. That's when they really needed me the most. But now I had the chance to be there for my grandkids - yes, grandkids. God let me live to see my grandbabies. I had to ask them to forgive me for all I had taken them through, the shame I had caused them, and the hurt I put them through. I started going to church on a regular basis to give God the praise for what He had done. I am forever thankful for my deliverance. I knew that it was God because the pain was gone. The guilt I felt because I thought what happened to me was my fault was gone too. God has a way of turning all bad things into good things.

At first, I was letting my kids talk to me any kind of way because I felt guilty. I didn't think I had a right to correct them because of my past. God let me know, "You owe your kids nothing but to ask them for their forgiveness." The enemy wasn't through with me yet. He started using my kids to hurt me. He had me thinking that me and my kids got along better when I used crack. I had to put my feet on that devil's neck and head, stomp him, and order him back to the pits of hell where he came from in Jesus' name because the blood of Jesus covers me.

When people I used to get high with saw me, they looked at me funny. They wondered how I went from looking like the walking dead two weeks ago to the level of restoration they saw now. They couldn't believe their eyes – *I now looked like I had something to live for.* When they commented, "Girl, you look good. How did you do it?" I was certain to reply, "Nobody but God. I give all the glory, honor, and praise to God because without Him I wouldn't be here today." They were shocked. They knew something changed in me; they just weren't sure how. But I knew it was only God who could have done this great transformation in my life. God completely made me over in a two-week period.

People commonly say, "God won't put more on you then you can bear." But to be honest, we sometimes put things on ourselves that are too much to bear. Don't get me wrong, God will help you through it. You will also be tested after He delivers you, so don't be surprised.

I lived with my oldest daughter, and it was now time for me to get out on my own. I applied for a housing project. They said it would take up to a year but how many of you know when God is with you, who can be against you?

What then shall we say to these things? If
God is for us, who can be against us?
-Romans 8:31

I got my house within nine months. They
moved me right into the same area where I first
started getting high. I thought, *Come on God, for
real? But how many know, when God does
anything, He does it right, and He will get the
glory? Amen.*

I lived there for three years. I saw people I
used to get high with, all the way back from
1986. Some of them were still getting high, some
weren't. But through it all, God got the glory by
me being a living testimony. I thank God for His
Grace. Amen.

Luke 20:43 says, "Till I make Your enemies
Your footstool." My enemy was crack cocaine,
and I used it as my footstool. I stepped up on it
and moved higher in Christ, Amen. *I moved on
up a little higher.*

The devil still fought me from the north, east,
south, and west, but I refused to move. I believed
God and stood on His word:

Yet in all these things we are more than
conquerors through Him who loved us.
-Romans 8:37

Even when I was in the world, I kept His word in my mouth and in my heart. Now, it was time to *use* it against the devil. I said, "God, You said I'm the head and not the tail. I shall be above and not beneath." As I used the word, he stopped messing with me.

> And the Lord will make you the head and not the tail; you shall be above only, and not be beneath, if you heed the commandments of the Lord your God, which I command you today, and are careful to observe *them*.
>
> -Deuteronomy 28:13

9

Fight to Win

The devil started to use my own children to say things like, "You didn't raise me. You can't tell me what to do." They talked back and wanted to fight. It was the worst. I didn't let it stop my deliverance, though. I gave my kids to God. I know it was Him who gave them to me, and He knows them better than I do.

> You are of God, little children, and have overcome them, because He who is in you is greater than he who is in the world.
> -1 John 4:4

I was in and out of jail because I continued to drive with a suspended license. I know I was wrong. The funniest thing about it was when I was on drugs, I never got pulled over.

God cleaned me up. I got a job with my sister and her husband at their restaurant and was going to church. The enemy was on my trail and tried to keep me from going to church.

After I got my license back, they turned right around and took it again. I was crying and asking

God, "Why? Even after I paid $800, my license was revoked for five years." What the devil meant for my bad, God turned around for my good and His glory. Instead of waiting five years, I got my license back in one year. I say this to show you how God works, even in the little everyday things, like helping get a license back. You have to realize, God has the last say so on your life, in your life, and about your life.

God is still working in my life. When you trust in God, make Him first in your life, allow Him to lead you, and follow & obey Him, you can't go wrong.

He sent from above, He took me;
He drew me out of many waters.
He delivered me from my strong enemy,
From those who hated me,
For they were too strong for me.
They confronted me in the day of my calamity,
But the LORD was my support.
He also brought me out into a broad place;
He delivered me because He delighted in me.

-Psalm 18:16-19

He delivered me from drugs, problems, pain, sickness, self-pity, strongholds, and all my enemies. Keep your hope and focus on God and you will experience His saving grace and mercy every time.

Even in your deepest waters, God will hold on to your hands to keep you from drowning in the sea of *issues*. I know it to be true. As I look back over my life, I know I was drowning, and going down for the third time before death. God reached down and took me out of my deepest waters, gave me mouth-to-mouth resuscitation, and blew life back into me.

Prayer:

God, I pray for those who find themselves in deep water. Let them ask for Your life jacket of freedom, hope, and love; especially those who do not know Your saving grace and love.

Amen.

10

God's Healing Power; Miracle Worker

I started getting sick. My blood pressure was up, my blood count was low, I was getting blood transfusions at least once a month, and I had a mini stroke. I underwent a hysterectomy to keep from losing additional blood and stayed in the hospital for almost a week. The devil was trying to kill me . . . *But God.*

When you know who you are and whom you belong to, a change takes place to your life. With the Lord's help, I got better. I moved into a nice three-bedroom, two full bath house, with a screened patio, in Port St. John, FL. God had moved me up from project housing, where I first started smoking and getting high, from across the road where drugs were sold, into a house in a nice area. When we are thankful for the little things, God will bless us with better. My house was ten minutes from the church. I lived there for about a year and a half.

I started getting sick again. They didn't know what was going on with me, other than a blood pressure issue. My daughter came home from Germany in July to pick up her two boys. Let me show you how God takes care of His children, even in the midst of sin (grace). I went to Texas where she was stationed. I stayed there for three months. My head continued to hurt, but I was doing okay.

I came home just in time for my other baby girl to give birth to her little girl, her first child, on November 6, 2014. The sickness started up again once I was home. My blood pressure was up, the headaches intensified, and I found out I had another mini stroke. They found three aneurysms. The local hospital didn't do the type of surgery they said I needed, so I was sent several hours away to a hospital in Gainesville, FL. This hospital said they didn't see anything. I thank God for my healing! God will look out for you even when you can't look after yourself. God knows just what doctors he wants you to go to, and the one that is not for you.

I continued to battle headaches. They became so *tight*, I couldn't take it anymore. I went back to the hospital. When I told them what the hospital in Gainesville told me, they said it can't be true. They made an appointment for me with another doctor.

Before the day of the appointment came, I got sick again. I went to a different hospital in my county. They saw three aneurysms, too. They were going to try to coil them, but they couldn't because of the way they were shaped. They planned to go inside my brain and clamp them instead. I was in the hospital for about a week. When they discussed the operation with me, they went over the cons: I could lose my memory; I could have a stroke during the operation; and I might die. The pro, with prayer, was everything is going to be alright.

Thankfully, God gave me praying doctors. The Bible tells us healing is the children's bread (*see* Mark 7: 24-30).

... "If you diligently heed the voice of the Lord your God and do what is right in His sight, give ear to His commandments and keep all His statutes, I will put none of the diseases on you which I have brought on the Egyptians. For I am the Lord who heals you."

-Exodus 15:26

I can't honestly say, I wasn't scared because I was. I did know for certain, in whatever was going to happen, God had the last say so. I prayed:

God, I thank you for everything. I mean everything that is going on with me. There's a reason for this and a purpose. You are my Way Maker. You have been better to me than I've been to myself. I lay here in this hospital bed with wondering thoughts. In about two and a half hours from now, I'll be having surgery. I know everything is in Your hands, but I am also human and right now I'm a bit on edge. So, as they put me under, God I know You are on top of everything. I know You haven't brought me this far to leave me now. My faith in You makes me strong. I'm leaning on You so I can't go wrong. I know in my heart, You won't leave me alone. I ask You to wrap Your loving arms around my kids and family. Give them peace of mind, knowing You have it all in Your control.

Amen.

"Return and tell Hezekiah the leader of My people, 'Thus says the Lord, the God of David your father: "I have heard your prayer, I have seen your tears; surely I will heal you. On the third day you shall go up to the house of the Lord.

-2 Kings 20:5

Heal me, O Lord, and I shall be healed; Save me, and I shall be saved, For You are my praise.

-Jeremiah 17:14

God not only brought me through the surgery, but He kept me. See, when I was out there doing drugs, I didn't go to the doctor. All the while, those aneurysms were ticking time bombs ready to explode at any given moment. . . *But God.* They could have ruptured when I was out there, but God didn't allow them to. He cleaned me up and waited six years until I went to Texas and was rested. He knew this time was coming.

God will take you through, help you through, and see you through - just trust in Him. Right now, in my life, I can truly say I'm free from drugs, alcohol, sleeping around, lying, stealing, and cigarettes. When I let God take control of my life, meaning I put my life in His hands, from that day to this one a great deliverance and restoration took place. I am saved and Holy host filled. Jesus is my Lord and Savior.

Don't be ashamed of what you did in your past nor what happened to you; abandonment, molestation, mental, physical, and / or emotional abuse. Shame keeps us down and bound instead of believing and available for deliverance. When we keep things locked inside of us, we unintentionally lock God out. I encourage you, *Let Go & Let God*. He is a forgiving God.

Waiting for people to forgive you will keep you down. Sometimes people say they forgive you, but as soon as they get mad, they throw it back up in your face, no matter who it is. Once God forgives you, He puts it in the sea of forgetfulness and never remembers nor speaks of it again (*see* Micah 7:19). And, "As far as the east is from the west, so far has He removed our transgressions from us" (Psalm 103:12). The only people who keep bringing it up are us and the devil.

To those of you who are reading this book, know God has no special person, we are all His

special people. The things He has done for me,
He will also do the same for you.

God bless you, Amen!

And we know that all things work
together for good to those who love God,
to those who are the called according to
His purpose.

-Romans 8:28

And the Lord will make you the head and
not the tail; you shall be above only, and
not be beneath, if you heed the
commandments of the Lord your God,
which I command you today, and are
careful to observe *them*.

-Deuteronomy 28:13

My Engineer

Jesus is my engineer.
He fixed my life like a highway,
making sure my roads are clear
to travel on keeping me from
going down dead-ends.

I was traveling down
dead-end roads.
I went down to Alcohol Lane.
Turned left on Cigarette Circle.
And another left on Drug Alley.
I had nowhere else I could go,
no one I could turn to.

But then my engineer stepped in
and had me turn right onto
highway to Heaven Lane.
I turned right onto
Eternal Life Street.

These roads are expensive.
You have to give up everything,
in order to get to Golden Gate Road.
It's always exciting to travel on
a new road when you know
where you're going to end up
- at Jesus Palace.

By Dorothea

www.ingramcontent.com/pod-product-compliance
Lightning Source LLC
Chambersburg PA
CBHW070927120626
46546CB00004B/1372